Especially for

_____

From

_____

Date

_____

© 2006 by Barbour Publishing, Inc.

ISBN 978-1-61626-134-4

Compiled by Joanie Garborg.

Quotes without an attribution are by anonymous or unknown authors.

Published by Barbour Publishing, Inc., P.O. Box 719, Uhrichsville, Ohio 44683, www.barbourbooks.com

Our mission is to publish and distribute inspirational products offering exceptional value and biblical encouragement to the masses.

Member of the
Evangelical Christian
Publishers Association

Printed in China.

365 Stress-Free Moments
for Women

BARBOUR
PUBLISHING

Praise God for all that is past.
Trust Him for all that is to come.

January 2

Life itself cannot give you joy
unless you really will it.
Life just gives you time and space—
it's up to you to fill it.

December 31

Home, the spot of earth supremely blest, a dearer, sweeter spot than all the rest.

ROBERT MONTGOMERY

January 3

May gentle and beautiful
moments be yours today.

December 30

May God, who puts all things together,
makes all things whole. . .make us into
what gives him most pleasure, by means
of the sacrifice of Jesus, the Messiah.
All glory to Jesus forever and always!

Hebrews 13:20–21 msg

January 4

None are more blessed than
those who think they are.

December 29

Every step is an end,
and every step is a fresh beginning.
JOHANN WOLFGANG VON GOETHE

January 5

My life flows on in endless song;
Above earth's lamentation
I hear the sweet though far-off hymn
That hails a new creation. . . .
Since God is Lord of heaven and earth,
How can I keep from singing?

December 28

May your hours of reminiscence
be filled with days of good cheer
and weeks of pleasant memories.

January 6

Blessed is she who is too busy to worry in the daytime and too sleepy to worry at night.

I swam ten laps, I ran three miles,
I biked seven miles. . . . It's been a good year!

An instant of pure love is more precious to
God. . .than all other good works together, even
though it may seem as if nothing were done.

ST. JOHN OF THE CROSS

December 26

Invite a miracle into your life.
They are everywhere, all around you,
and too often go unnoticed.

January 8

God is the one who enables us to find joy in this moment—just as it is, just as we are.

"The joy of the LORD is your strength."

NEHEMIAH 8:10 NIV

December 25

Many merry Christmases, many happy
New Years. Unbroken friendships, great
accumulations of cheerful recollections and
affections on earth, and heaven for us all.

CHARLES DICKENS

Any time you think you have influence, try ordering around someone else's dog.

December 24

"Behold, the virgin shall be with child
and shall bear a Son, and they shall
call His name Immanuel," which
translated means, "God with us."

MATTHEW 1:23 NASB

Life is like a mirror—we get the
best results when we smile at it.

The Lord from Heaven,
Born of a village girl, carpenter's son.
Wonderful, Prince of Peace,
The mighty God.

ALFRED TENNYSON

If Winter comes, can Spring be far behind?

Percy Bysshe Shelley

December 22

All the great purposes of God culminate in Him. The greatest and most momentous fact which the history of the world records is the fact of His birth.

CHARLES SPURGEON

January 12

Cheerfulness brings sunshine to the soul and drives away the shadows of anxiety.

Hannah Whitall Smith

December 21

Love came down at Christmas,
Love all lovely, love divine;
Love was born at Christmas,
Star and angels gave the sign.

CHRISTINA ROSSETTI

It's usually through our hard times,
the unexpected and not-according-to-plan times,
that we experience God in more intimate ways.
We discover an unquenchable
longing to know Him more.

December 20

Every heart comes home for Christmas.

January 14

It is pleasing to God whenever you rejoice or laugh from the bottom of your heart.

MARTIN LUTHER

Heap on more wood!
The wind is chill;
But let it whistle as it will,
We'll keep our Christmas merry still.

WALTER SCOTT

Learn from the mistakes of others;
you don't have enough time
to make them all yourself.

December 18

The most precious gifts are wrapped in love.

January 16

Always be in a state of expectancy, and see that
you leave room for God to come in as He likes.

OSWALD CHAMBERS

December 17

How silently,
How silently the wondrous gift is given.
So God imparts to human hearts
The wonders of His heaven.

PHILLIPS BROOKS

Do not forget little kindnesses,
and do not remember small faults.

CHINESE PROVERB

December 16

The best of all is God with us!
JOHN WESLEY

When all is said and done, the last word
is Immanuel—God-With-Us.
ISAIAH 8:10 MSG

January 18

That I am here is a wonderful mystery
to which I will respond with joy.

December 15

Where others see but the dawn coming over the hill, I see the soul of God shouting for joy.

WILLIAM BLAKE

What matters is not your outer appearance—the
styling of your hair, the jewelry you wear,
the cut of your clothes—but your inner
disposition. Cultivate inner beauty, the gentle,
gracious kind that God delights in.

1 PETER 3:3–4 MSG

December 14

Christmas is a time of the heart, not just a date.
Its meaning transcends time. Jesus was born to
love us and fill our lives with Himself.

January 20

This life is not all. It is an "unfinished symphony". . .with those who know that they are related to God and have felt "the power of an endless life."

HENRY WARD BEECHER

December 13

Joyful, all ye nations rise,
Join the triumph of the skies;
With the angelic host proclaim,
"Christ is born in Bethlehem!"

CHARLES WESLEY

January 21

Work for the Lord. The pay isn't much,
but His retirement plan is out of this world.

My heart took delight in all my work,
and this was the reward for all my labor.
ECCLESIASTES 2:10 NIV

December 12

For unto us a child is born, unto us a son is
given: and the government shall be upon
his shoulder: and his name shall be called
Wonderful, Counsellor, The mighty God, The
everlasting Father, The Prince of Peace.

Isaiah 9:6 KJV

January 22

[Cheerfulness] is to know that God holds
all things in His control and that
He neither slumbers nor sleeps.

HANNAH WHITALL SMITH

We are of such value to God that He came to live among us. . .and to guide us home. He will go to any length to seek us, even to being lifted high upon the cross to draw us back to Himself. We can only respond by loving God for His love.

CATHERINE OF SIENA

January 23

When I think upon my God,
my heart is so full of joy that the notes
dance and leap from my pen.

FRANZ JOSEF HAYDN

My heart leaps for joy and
I will give thanks to him in song.

PSALM 28:7 NIV

December 10

Hem your blessings
with praise, lest they unravel.

January 24

Begin where you are, but don't stay there.

December 9

Love is the true means by which
the world is enjoyed: our love to others
and others' love to us.

THOMAS TRAHERNE

The nicest thing we can do for our heavenly
Father is to be kind to one of His children.

ST. TERESA OF AVILA

December 8

We are ever so secure in the everlasting arms.

The eternal God is your refuge,
and underneath are the everlasting arms.

DEUTERONOMY 33:27 NIV

January 26

Into all our lives, in many simple, familiar, homely ways, God infuses this element of joy from the surprises of life, which unexpectedly brighten our days and fill our eyes with light.

HENRY WADSWORTH LONGFELLOW

December 7

Even the most spectacular field owes its charm
to the beauty of each individual blossom.

KELLY EILEEN HAKE

The shadows are behind you if
you walk toward the light.

December 6

Live your life while you have it. Life is a splendid gift—there is nothing small about it.

FLORENCE NIGHTINGALE

January 28

We are so preciously loved by God that we cannot even comprehend it. No created being can ever know how much and how sweetly and tenderly God loves them.

ST. JULIAN OF NORWICH

December 5

Our true character comes out in the way we pray.

OSWALD CHAMBERS

We're in charge of the effort.
God will handle the results.

December 4

God does not give Himself to us fully
until we fully give ourselves to Him.
TERESA OF AVILA

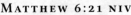

For where your treasure is,
there your heart will be also.
MATTHEW 6:21 NIV

January 30

You always find what you are looking for
in the last place you look.

❋

God. . .doesn't play hide-and-seek with us.
He's not remote; he's near.

ACTS 17:27 MSG

December 3

God loves each one of us as if
there were only one of us.

AUGUSTINE

A happy heart is the best service
we can give to God.

December 2

There is not a heart but has its
moments of longing, yearning for something
better, nobler, holier than it knows now.

HENRY WARD BEECHER

February 1

When we start to count flowers,
we cease to count weeds;
When we start to count blessings,
we cease to count needs;
When we start to count laughter,
we cease to count tears;
When we start to count memories,
we cease to count years.

December 1

For you know the grace of our Lord Jesus Christ,
that though he was rich, yet for your sakes
he became poor, so that you through
his poverty might become rich.

2 CORINTHIANS 8:9 NIV

You are not old unless you
get wrinkles in your heart.

November 30

A smile costs nothing but gives much.
It takes but a moment, but the memory
of it sometimes lasts forever.

February 3

If you have to start over,
have a friend by your side.

Yesterday is gone. Tomorrow has not yet come.
We only have today. Let us begin.

MOTHER TERESA

February 4

We walk without fear, full of hope and courage
and strength to do His will, waiting for the
endless good which He is always giving as fast as
He can get us to take it in.

GEORGE MACDONALD

How beautiful it is to do nothing—
and then to rest afterward.

SPANISH PROVERB

February 5

One day I'll look back on all this and laugh.

There is a time for everything. . .a time
to weep and a time to laugh.

ECCLESIASTES 3:1, 4 NIV

A well-informed person is somebody who has
the same views and opinions as mine.

February 6

My great concern is not whether God is on our side; my great concern is to be on God's side.

ABRAHAM LINCOLN

November 26

Nostalgia is the realization that things weren't
as unbearable as they seemed to be at the time.

February 7

It is of immense importance to
learn to laugh at ourselves.

KATHERINE MANSFIELD

I will say of the Lord, "He is my refuge and
my fortress, my God, in whom I trust". . . . A
thousand may fall at your side, ten thousand at
your right hand, but it will not come near you.

PSALM 91:2, 7 NIV

If we had no winter, the spring would not be so pleasant; if we did not sometimes taste of adversity, prosperity would not be so welcome.

ANNE BRADSTREET

November 24

You can be sure that God will take care of
everything you need, his generosity exceeding
even yours in the glory that pours from Jesus.
Our God and Father abounds in glory
that just pours out into eternity.

PHILIPPIANS 4:19–20 MSG

February 9

No one is useless in this world who
lightens the burdens of it for another.
CHARLES DICKENS

There's always something for
which to be thankful.

CHARLES DICKENS

Relaxation was God's idea.

GINA MASELLI

November 22

Grant me the power of saying things
too simple and too sweet for words.

COVENTRY PATMORE

February 11

There is no substitute for plain,
everyday goodness.
MALTBIE D. BABCOCK

❀

For this very reason, make every
effort to add to your faith goodness;
and to goodness, knowledge.
2 PETER 1:5 NIV

For health and food, for love and friends,
for everything Your goodness sends,
Father in Heaven, we thank You.

RALPH WALDO EMERSON

February 12

Keep praying, but be thankful that God's
answers are wiser than your prayers!
WILLIAM CULBERTSON

November 20

If we thank God for all the good things, we won't have time to complain about the bad.

In everything give thanks.

1 Thessalonians 5:18 nasb

February 13

A simple "I love you" will do. But a big "I love you" with a dozen roses would do better.

The darkest of nights displays the brilliance of
God's glory reflected in the stars.

Take time to laugh—it
is the music of the soul.

November 18

Always remember to forget the things
that made you sad. But never forget to
remember the things that made you glad.

ELBERT HUBBARD

February 15

One of life's mysteries is how a two-pound box
of candy can make a person gain five pounds.

My soul will be satisfied
as with the richest of foods;
with singing lips my mouth will praise you.

PSALM 63:5 NIV

God gives the very best to those
who leave the choice to Him.

February 16

Happiness is something that comes into our lives
through a door we don't remember leaving open.

November 16

Our chief end is to glorify
God and to enjoy Him forever.

PRESBYTERIAN CATECHISM

February 17

Every sunset brings the
promise of a new dawn.

People weigh our actions,
but God weighs our intentions.

February 18

We are all precious in His sight.

November 14

I'm thankful for work—but what
I'm really thankful for is payday.

"Be strong. Take heart. Payday is coming!"

2 CHRONICLES 15:7 MSG

February 19

When we fall asleep in prayer, God has
ways of reminding us to finish. (And you
thought the dogs were barking at the moon.)

November 13

A single grateful thought toward heaven
is the most perfect prayer.

G. E. LESSING

February 20

You can trust God right now to supply all your needs for today. And if your needs are more tomorrow, His supply will be greater also.

November 12

As we follow Him who is everlasting,
we will touch the things that last forever.

February 21

Happiness is a healthy mental attitude,
a grateful spirit, and a clear heart full of love.

November 11

Our heavenly Father never takes anything from His children unless He means to give them something better.

George MacDonald

Just as there comes a warm sunbeam into
every cottage window, so comes a love—born
of God's care for every separate need.

NATHANIEL HAWTHORNE

November 10

Hope for the best, be prepared for the worst,
and take what comes with a grin.

And hope does not disappoint us,
because God has poured out his love into
our hearts by the Holy Spirit.

ROMANS 5:5 NIV

February 23

Within each of us, just waiting to blossom,
is the wonderful promise of all we can be.

But for some trouble and sorrow, we should never know half the good there is about us.

CHARLES DICKENS

I would rather walk with God in
the dark than go alone in the light.

MARY GARDINER BRAINARD

November 8

You can get by on charm for about fifteen minutes. After that, you'd better know something.

February 25

With God, no one is ever lost in the crowd.

"If God gives such attention to the appearance of wildflowers—most of which are never even seen—don't you think he'll attend to you, take pride in you, do his best for you?"

MATTHEW 6:30 MSG

November 7

A bore is a person who persists in talking about himself when you want to talk about yourself.

Be gracious in your speech.
The goal is to bring out the best in others
in a conversation. . .not cut them out.

COLOSSIANS 4:6 MSG

February 26

When you get into a tight place and everything goes against you, 'til it seems as though you can not hang on a minute longer, never give up then, for that is just the place and time that the tide will turn.

HARRIET BEECHER STOWE

November 6

Every moment is full of wonder,
and God is always present.

February 27

You pay God a compliment by
asking great things of Him.

ST. TERESA OF AVILA

November 5

I am better than I was, but not quite
so good as I was before I got worse.

We also rejoice in our sufferings, because we
know that suffering produces perseverance;
perseverance, character; and character, hope.

ROMANS 5:3–4 NIV

February 28

Should we feel at times disheartened and
discouraged, a simple movement of
heart toward God will renew our powers. . . .
He will give us at the moment the
strength and courage that we need.

FRANÇOIS FÉNELON

November 4

I am glad that in the springtime of
life there were those who planted
flowers of love in my heart.

ROBERT LOUIS STEVENSON

March 1

A kind heart is a fountain of gladness, making everything in its vicinity freshen into smiles.

WASHINGTON IRVING

I belong to the "Great God Party" and will have nothing to do with the "Little God Party." Christ does not want nibblers of the possible, but grabbers of the impossible.

C. T. STUDD

Do not be anxious about anything, but in everything, by prayer and petition, with thanksgiving, present your requests to God.

PHILIPPIANS 4:6 NIV

November 2

Lord, I love You for being You. I love you for loving me. I love You for saving me, protecting me, revealing Yourself to me. You're awesome, God, marvelous and wonderful!

March 3

Each of us may be sure that if God sends us on stony paths, He will provide us with strong shoes, and He will not send us out on any journey for which He does not equip us well.

ALEXANDER MACLAREN

November 1

May God's love guide you through
the special plans He has for your life.

That load becomes light
which is cheerfully borne.

OVID

October 31

If God says it, you can stake your life upon it!

❋

You know with all your heart
and soul that not one of all the good
promises the Lord your God gave you has failed.
Every promise has been fulfilled.

Joshua 23:14 niv

March 5

Why is it that our memory is good enough to retain the least triviality that happens to us and yet not good enough to recollect how often we have told it to the same person?

FRANÇOIS DE LA ROCHEFOUCAULD

Let nothing disturb you; let nothing frighten you: Everything passes away except God; God alone is sufficient.

TERESA OF AVILA

March 6

I know what it is to be in need, and I know what
it is to have plenty. I have learned the secret of
being content in any and every situation.

PHILIPPIANS 4:12 NIV

October 29

I've learned that to be with those I like is enough.

WALT WHITMAN

March 7

If you have a special need today,
focus your full attention on the goodness
and greatness of your Father rather than
on the size of your need. Your need is so
small compared to His ability to meet it.

Sense of humor, God's great gift,
causes spirits to uplift;
Helps to make our bodies mend,
lightens burdens, cheers a friend;
Tickles children, elders grin
at this warmth that glows within;
Surely in the great hereafter,
heaven must be full of laughter!

God has a purpose for your life,
and no one else can take your place.

October 27

At the very heart of the universe is God's desire to love and to forgive.

March 9

Always do the right thing. This will
please some people and surprise the rest.

As we have opportunity, let us
do good to all people.

GALATIANS 6:10 NIV

October 26

If you fall on your face, look around.
You're probably in good company.

❃

It's better to have a partner than go it alone. . . .
And if one falls down, the other helps.

ECCLESIASTES 4:9–10 MSG

If all were rain and never sun,
No bow could span the hill;
If all were sun and never rain,
There'd be no rainbow still.

CHRISTINA ROSSETTI

October 25

God's grace keeps pace
with whatever we face.

March 11

The LORD is my shepherd;
I have everything I need.

PSALM 23:1 NLT

What we really are matters more
than what others say we are.

Every heart that has beat strong and cheerfully
has left a hopeful impulse behind it in the world
and bettered the tradition of mankind.

ROBERT LOUIS STEVENSON

October 23

God is, indeed, a wonderful Father
who longs to pour out His mercy upon us—
and whose majesty is so great that He
can transform us from deep within.

TERESA OF AVILA

March 13

Every person you meet is
an opportunity for kindness.

Friendship is the golden thread
that ties all hearts together.

March 14

A miracle is where the hand
of God is obvious.

Now faith is the substance of things hoped for,
the evidence of things not seen.

HEBREWS 11:1 KJV

October 21

May God give you eyes to see beauty
only the heart can understand.

March 15

All things bright and beautiful,
All creatures great and small,
All things wise and wonderful,
The Lord God made them all.

CECIL FRANCES ALEXANDER

October 20

When the going gets tough, the tough get going.
The not-so-tough scream for help.

Hear my prayer, O LORD; let my
cry for help come to you.

PSALM 102:1 NIV

God gave me friends so I
wouldn't have to laugh alone.

October 19

We live by admiration, hope, and love.
WILLIAM WORDSWORTH

March 17

All of us could take a lesson from the weather.
It pays no attention to criticism.

May the dazzling rays of the sunshine of
God's love reach through the clouds of
your life and brighten up your skies.

A sunset is heaven's gate ajar.

October 17

Without God, I can't;
without me, God won't.

AUGUSTINE

March 19

You will reach your destination
if you walk with God.

Take me by the hand;
lead me down the path of truth.

PSALM 25:5 MSG

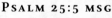

When we are told that God, who is our dwelling place, is also our fortress, it can only mean one thing. . .that if we will but live in our dwelling place, we shall be perfectly safe and secure.

HANNAH WHITALL SMITH

March 20

I know not where His islands lift
their fronded palms in air;
I only know I cannot drift
beyond His love and care.

JOHN GREENLEAF WHITTIER

October 15

There is no safer place to be than
in the Father's hands.

March 21

Laughter is like changing a baby's diaper—it doesn't permanently solve any problems, but it makes things more acceptable for a while.

May our Lord Jesus Christ. . .encourage
your hearts and strengthen you
in every good deed and word.

2 THESSALONIANS 2:16–17 NIV

In His arms He carries us all day long.

FANNY CROSBY

October 13

Use what talents you possess: The woods would be very silent if no birds sang there except those that sang best.

HENRY VAN DYKE

March 23

God has always used ordinary people to
carry out His extraordinary mission.

"Nothing is impossible with God."

LUKE 1:37 NIV

I am not what I ought to be; I am not what I wish to be; I am not what I hope to be; but, by the grace of God, I am not what I was.

JOHN NEWTON

We may be surprised at whom
God sends to answer our prayers.

October 11

The riches that are in the heart cannot be stolen.
RUSSIAN PROVERB

March 25

May God grant you peace. And may you know
that peace isn't a pot of gold rewarded to you
after chasing some rainbow's end—it's a gift.

There's sunshine in your smile!

The happiness of your life depends
upon the character of your thoughts.

October 9

All of God's revealed truths are sealed until they are opened to us through obedience. Even the smallest bit of obedience opens heaven.

OSWALD CHAMBERS

March 27

If at first you don't succeed,
see if the loser gets anything.

Commit to the LORD whatever you do,
and your plans will succeed.

PROVERBS 16:3 NIV

Work like you don't need the money,
love like you've never been hurt,
and dance like no one is watching.

Worrying is like a rocking chair;
it gives you something to do, but
it doesn't get you anywhere.

October 7

Our best friends know the worst
about us but refuse to believe it.

Friends love through all kinds of weather.

PROVERBS 17:17 MSG

March 29

Exuberance is beauty.

WILLIAM BLAKE

October 6

A cheerful heart fills the day with song.

PROVERBS 15:15 MSG

Character may be manifested in the great
moments, but it is made in the small ones.

PHILLIPS BROOKS

October 5

Humility is like underwear—essential,
but indecent if you show it off.

March 31

Give me a sense of humor, and
I will find happiness in life.

THOMAS MORE

October 4

When you are lonely, I wish you love;
When you are down, I wish you joy;
When you are troubled, I wish you peace;
When things are complicated,
I wish you simple beauty;
When things are chaotic, I wish you inner silence;
At all times I wish you the God of hope.

It is better to give than to lend,
and it costs about the same.
BENJAMIN FRANKLIN

October 3

The consciousness of loving and
being loved brings a warmth and richness
to life that nothing else can bring.

OSCAR WILDE

April 2

You have made us for Yourself, O Lord,
and our hearts are restless until they rest in You.

AUGUSTINE

Appreciation is like salt—a little goes a long way to bring out the best in us.

April 3

It is enough that we have Christ's direction.
The light will break in God's own time.

Wisdom will enter your heart, and knowledge
will be pleasant to your soul.

PROVERBS 2:10 NIV

October 1

Seeds of kindness will yield
a bountiful harvest of blessing.

April 4

The splendor of the rose and the whiteness
of the lily do not rob the little violet of its
scent nor the daisy of its simple charm.
If every tiny flower wanted to be a rose,
spring would lose its loveliness.

THERESE OF LISIEUX

It is the morning of your
life—the best is yet to be.

April 5

May you be ever-present in
the garden of God's love.

September 29

Those who love are borne on wings;
they run and are filled with joy; they are free
and unrestricted. . . . Beyond all things
they rest in the one highest thing,
from Whom streams all that is good.

THOMAS À KEMPIS

April 6

The soul should always stand ajar, ready
to welcome the ecstatic experience.

EMILY DICKINSON

To do great and important tasks, two things are necessary: a plan and not quite enough time.

Look backward—see Christ dying for you.
Look upward—see Christ pleading for you.
Look inward—see Christ living in you.
Look forward—see Christ coming for you.

September 27

God shall be my hope, my stay,
my guide, and lantern to my feet.

WILLIAM SHAKESPEARE

April 8

Charity yields high returns.

ECCLESIASTES 11:1 MSG

A closed mouth gathers no feet.

❉

Watch the way you talk. . . . Say
only what helps, each word a gift.

EPHESIANS 4:29 MSG

Gratitude is the expression of
enjoyment of God and His gifts.

September 25

When you have. . .accomplished your daily task,
go to sleep in peace. God is awake.

VICTOR HUGO

April 10

And He departed from our sight that we
might return to our heart and there find Him.
For He departed and, behold, He is here.

AUGUSTINE

God put me on earth to accomplish
a certain number of things. Right now
I am so far behind, I will never die.

If you can't get people to listen to you
any other way, tell them it's confidential.

September 23

If it weren't for the last minute,
nothing would get done.

April 12

The cross is the only ladder high enough
to touch the threshold of heaven.

GEORGE DANA BOARDMAN

That Hand which bears all nature up
Shall guard His children well.

WILLIAM COWPER

April 13

Only some of us can learn by
other people's mistakes. The rest of
us have to be the other people.

Above all and before all, do this: Get Wisdom!

PROVERBS 4:7 MSG

September 21

Keep close to your rule, the Word of God,
and to your guide, the Spirit of God,
and never be afraid of expecting too much.
JOHN WESLEY

April 14

Most of us don't realize how much we have to be
thankful for until we have to pay taxes on it.

September 20

My mind not only wanders,
sometimes it leaves completely.

And should I wander off like a lost sheep—seek
me! I'll recognize the sound of your voice.

PSALM 119:176 MSG

Great acts of love are done by those who are habitually performing small acts of kindness.

September 19

The really happy person is one who
can enjoy the scenery on a detour.

April 16

The great Easter truth is not that we are to live newly after death, but that we are to be new here and now by the power of the Resurrection.

PHILLIPS BROOKS

Never make a principle out of your experience;
let God be as original with
other people as He is with you.

OSWALD CHAMBERS

Dream of the person you would like to be, but remember that God won't waste the person you are.

September 17

A candle loses nothing of its light
by lighting another candle.

April 18

A good laugh makes us better friends
with ourselves and everybody around us.

ORISON SWETT MARDEN

September 16

O Lord, Thou knowest how busy
I must be today; if I forget Thee,
do not Thou forget me. . . . Amen.

JACOB ASTLEY

Before the mountains were born or you brought forth the earth and the world, from everlasting to everlasting you are God.

PSALM 90:2 NIV

September 15

Nothing can compare to the beauty and greatness of the soul in which our King dwells in His full majesty.

TERESA OF AVILA

April 20

The year's at the spring
And day's at the morn. . .
God's in His heaven—
All's right with the world!

ROBERT BROWNING

Blessed are they who can laugh at themselves,
for they shall never cease to be amused.

April 21

There are some friends you know
you will have for the rest of your life.
You're welded together by love, trust, respect,
loss—or simple embarrassment.

Friends come and friends go,
but a true friend sticks by you like family.

PROVERBS 18:24 MSG

September 13

To forgive means to surrender
your right to get even.

❋

Forgive one another as quickly and
thoroughly as God in Christ forgave you.

Ephesians 4:32 MSG

April 22

The best way to succeed in life is to act
on the advice we give to others.

September 12

Life is short, and we never have enough time for the hearts of those who travel the way with us. Oh, be swift to love! Make haste to be kind.

Henri Frédéric Amiel

When Christ ascended
triumphantly,
from star to star,
He left the gates of heaven ajar.

HENRY WADSWORTH LONGFELLOW

September 11

Finish each day and be done with it.
You have done what you could. . . . Tomorrow
is a new day; you shall begin it serenely
and with too high a spirit to be
encumbered with your old nonsense.

RALPH WALDO EMERSON

April 24

Cheerfulness is the habit of
looking at the good side of things.

W. B. ULLATHORNE

If I were two-faced,
would I be wearing this one?
ABRAHAM LINCOLN

Were there no God, we would be in this glorious world with grateful hearts and no one to thank.

CHRISTINA ROSSETTI

September 9

"I'll take the hand of those who don't know the way, who can't see where they're going. I'll be a personal guide to them, directing them through unknown country. I'll be right there to show them what roads to take."

ISAIAH 42:16 MSG

April 26

By perseverance the snail reached the ark.

CHARLES H. SPURGEON

September 8

Never lose an opportunity of seeing anything that is beautiful; for beauty is God's handwriting—a wayside sacrament. Welcome it in every fair face, in every fair sky, in every fair flower, and thank God for it as a cup of blessing.

RALPH WALDO EMERSON

A blossom cannot tell what becomes of its fragrance as it drifts away, just as you cannot tell what becomes of your influence as you continue through life.

September 7

To have good relationships, the best rule is to keep your heart a little softer than your head.

April 28

You have no strength but what God gives, and you can have all the strength that God can give.

ANDREW MURRAY

September 6

Once you've accumulated sufficient knowledge
to get by, you're too old to remember it.

Bless the LORD, O my soul,
and forget not all his benefits.

PSALM 103:2 KJV

April 29

It takes both the sun and the rain to make a rainbow.

September 5

God's care for us is more watchful
and more tender than the care of any
human father could possibly be.

HANNAH WHITALL SMITH

April 30

The winter is past; the rains are over and gone.
Flowers appear on the earth;
the season of singing has come.

SONG OF SONGS 2:11–12 NIV

I pray thee, O God, that I
may be beautiful within.

SOCRATES

Character is doing the right thing
when no one is looking.

September 3

The attitude within is more important than the circumstances without.

May 2

Spring unlocks the flowers
to paint the laughing soil.

September 2

Bidden or unbidden, God is present.

I look behind me and you're there, then up
ahead and you're there, too—your reassuring
presence, coming and going. This is too much,
too wonderful—I can't take it all in!

PSALM 139:5–6 MSG

May 3

"Be still, and know that I am God."

PSALM 46:10 NIV

September 1

God did not tell us to follow Him because
He needed our help, but because He
knew that loving Him would make us whole.

IRENAEUS

May 4

God understands our prayers even when
we can't find the words to say them.

August 31

The glory is not in never failing,
but in rising every time you fail.

CHINESE PROVERB

Spring—
Now the woods are in leaf;
now the year is in its greatest beauty.

VIRGIL

August 30

True serenity comes when
we give ourselves to God.

ELLYN SANNA

May 6

The person who can make
others laugh is blessed.

When the soul has laid down its faults at the feet of God, it feels as though it had wings.

EUGENIE DE GUERIN

As God loveth a cheerful giver,
so He also loveth a cheerful taker. . .who takes
hold on His gifts with a glad heart.

JOHN DONNE

August 28

Happiness is as a butterfly which, when pursued,
is always beyond our grasp—but which, if you
will sit down quietly, may alight upon you.

NATHANIEL HAWTHORNE

May 8

The word *May* is a perfumed word. . . . It means youth, love, song, and all that is beautiful in life.

HENRY WADSWORTH LONGFELLOW

August 27

I have photographic memory. Unfortunately, it only offers same-day service.

Do not conform any longer to the pattern
of this world, but be transformed
by the renewing of your mind.

ROMANS 12:2 NIV

August 26

Friendships multiply joys and divide griefs.

HENRY GEORGE BOHN

May 10

Joy is the echo of God's life within us.

JOSEPH MARMION

The trouble with doing something right the first time is that nobody appreciates how difficult it was.

May 11

Everything around me may change,
but my God is changeless!

August 24

The best things are nearest: breath in
your nostrils, light in your eyes, flowers
at your feet, duties at your hand, the path of
Right just before you. Do not grasp at the stars,
but do life's plain common work as it comes,
certain that daily duties and daily bread
are the sweetest things in life.

ROBERT LOUIS STEVENSON

May 12

Everyone has a unique role to fill in the world
and is important in some respect.
Everyone, including and perhaps
especially you, is indispensable.

NATHANIEL HAWTHORNE

August 23

Be faithful in the little things,
for in them our strength lies.

MOTHER TERESA

When your work speaks for
itself, don't interrupt!

August 22

If you can't go around it, over it, or through it, you had better negotiate with it!

May 14

May God send His love like sunshine
in His warm and gentle way
to fill each corner of your heart
each moment of today.

Every person's life is a fairy
tale written by God's fingers.

HANS CHRISTIAN ANDERSEN

May 15

Prayer is the place where
burdens change shoulders.

May the God of hope fill you with all joy and peace
in believing, so that you will abound in hope.

ROMANS 15:13 NASB

August 20

Delight yourself in the LORD;
and He will give you the desires of your heart.

PSALM 37:4 NASB

May 16

Each little flower that opens,
Each little bird that sings—
God made their glowing colors;
He made their tiny wings.

<small>CECIL FRANCES ALEXANDER</small>

August 19

Because of His boundless love,
He became what we are in order that
He might make us what He is.

IRENAEUS

Today's bright moments are
tomorrow's fond memories.

August 18

I asked God for all things, that I might enjoy life.
He gave me life that I might enjoy all things.

May 18

For in the true nature of things, if we will rightly consider, every green tree is far more glorious than if it were made of gold and silver.

<small>MARTIN LUTHER</small>

Where there is faith, there is love.
Where there is love, there is peace.
Where there is peace, there is God.
Where there is God, there is no need.

God moves in a mysterious way
His wonders to perform;
He plants His footsteps in the sea,
And rides upon the storm.

WILLIAM COWPER

August 16

Write it on your heart that every
day is the best day of the year.

RALPH WALDO EMERSON

May 20

But now that you've found you don't have to listen to sin tell you what to do, and have discovered the delight of listening to God telling you, what a surprise! A whole, healed, put-together life right now.

ROMANS 6:22 MSG

Never forget that if you're headed in the wrong direction, God allows U-turns.

People may forget a word of wisdom,
but they never forget a word of kindness.

August 14

Faith is the daring of the soul
to go farther than it can see.

May 22

Little deeds of kindness,
Little words of love,
Help to make earth happy
Like the heaven above.

Julia Fletcher Carney

August 13

If I can be of any help,
you're in more trouble than I thought.

He comes alongside us when we go through
hard times, and before you know it, he brings
us alongside someone else who is going through
hard times so that we can be there for that
person just as God was there for us.

2 CORINTHIANS 1:4 MSG

God's fingers can touch nothing
but to mold it into loveliness.
GEORGE MacDONALD

August 12

Where the soul is full of peace and joy,
outward surroundings and circumstances
are of comparatively little account.

HANNAH WHITALL SMITH

May 24

Joyfulness keeps the heart and face young.

ORISON SWETT MARDEN

August 11

What does not kill me makes me stronger.

JOHANN WOLFGANG VON GOETHE

May 25

The miracles of nature do not seem miracles because they are so common. If no one had ever seen a flower, even a dandelion would be the most startling creation in the world.

August 10

We are sowing the flowers
of tomorrow in the seeds of today.

May 26

Any child can tell you that the sole purpose of a middle name is so he can tell when he's really in trouble.

August 9

Be kind to unkind people. It really gets to them.

✳

And be kind to one another, tender-hearted,
forgiving each other, just as God in
Christ also has forgiven you.

EPHESIANS 4:32 NASB

May 27

God's gifts put man's best dreams to shame.

ELIZABETH BARRETT BROWNING

August 8

I have learned to live each day as it comes and not to borrow trouble by dreading tomorrow.

DOROTHY DIX

May 28

We do not need to search for heaven over
here or over there in order to find our eternal
Father. In fact, we do not even need
to speak out loud, for though we speak in the
smallest whisper or the most fleeting thought,
He is close enough to hear us.

TERESA OF AVILA

August 7

God's help is nearer than the door.

IRISH PROVERB

May our God come and not keep silence.

PSALM 50:3 NASB

It is a big thing to do a little thing well.

August 6

Maybe the grass looks greener on the other side of the fence because they take care of it over there.

May 30

The soul is a temple, and God is silently building it by night and by day. Precious thoughts are building it, unselfish love is building it, all-penetrating faith is building it.

HENRY WARD BEECHER

August 5

Why should we live halfway up the hill and
swathed in the mists, when we might have
an unclouded sky and a radiant sun
over our heads if we would climb higher
and walk in the light of His face?

ALEXANDER MACLAREN

May 31

Beauty is in the eye of the beholder.
If those eyes are nearsighted, all the better.

❃

He has made everything beautiful in its time.
ECCLESIASTES 3:11 NIV

August 4

Don't fear tomorrow: God is already there.

Do not fear, for I am with you;
do not be dismayed, for I am your God.
I will strengthen you and help you.

ISAIAH 41:10 NIV

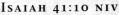

June 1

When we're conscious of the treasure of Himself
that God has placed in us, we're fully alive.

Tell people that there are 400 billion stars and they'll believe you. Tell them a bench has wet paint and they have to touch it.

In all ranks of life the human heart yearns for the beautiful; and the beautiful things that God makes are His gifts to all alike.

HARRIET BEECHER STOWE

August 2

Laughter is the gift of love, the music of the soul,
and the essence of humanity.

KELLY EILEEN HAKE

June 3

With the fearful strain that is on me night and day, if I did not laugh I should die.

<small>ABRAHAM LINCOLN</small>

I will lift up mine eyes unto the hills, from whence cometh my help. My help cometh from the LORD, which made heaven and earth.

PSALM 121:1–2 KJV

June 4

Let Jesus be in your heart,
Eternity in your spirit,
The world under your feet,
The will of God in your actions.
And let the love of God shine forth from you.
CATHERINE OF GENOA

July 31

Silence is golden when you
can't think of a good answer.

June 5

We have a God who
delights in impossibilities.

ANDREW MURRAY

July 30

Hope, like the gleaming taper's light,
Adorns and cheers our way;
And still, as darker grows the night,
Emits a lighter ray.

OLIVER GOLDSMITH

June 6

All the beautiful sentiments in the world weigh
less than a simple lovely action.

JAMES RUSSELL LOWELL

July 29

As a father has compassion on his children,
so the LORD has compassion on those who fear
him; for he knows how we are formed,
he remembers that we are dust.

PSALM 103:13–14 NIV

June 7

A prayer is a wish turned God-ward!
PHILLIPS BROOKS

Lord, may I and all who bear Your name,
by gentle love, Your truth proclaim.

June 8

God's suggestions will come to us—not so much commands from the outside as desires springing up within. They will originate in our will; we shall feel as though we desired to do so and so, not as though we must.

HANNAH WHITALL SMITH

July 27

A gentle word, like summer rain,
may soothe some heart and banish pain.
What joy or sadness often springs
from just the simple little things!

WILLA HOEY

June 9

Earth, with her thousand voices, praises God.

SAMUEL TAYLOR COLERIDGE

July 26

May you live all the days of your life.

JONATHAN SWIFT

Love GOD, your God. Walk in his ways. Keep his
commandments. . .so that you will live, really
live, live exuberantly, blessed by GOD, your God.

DEUTERONOMY 30:16 MSG

What the heart has once owned and had,
it shall never lose.

HENRY WARD BEECHER

July 25

Thank You, Lord, for this glorious world You have given us to enjoy. Thank You that You are with us, and Your power is all around us.

June 11

The trouble with work is—it's so daily.

Blessed be the Lord—day after
day he carries us along.

Psalm 68:19 MSG

July 24

Happiness consists more in small conveniences
or pleasures that occur every day than in
great pieces of good fortune that happen
but seldom to a man in the course of his life.

BENJAMIN FRANKLIN

Always remember you're unique,
just like everyone else.

July 23

You never can measure what God will do
through you. . . . Keep your relationship right
with Him. Then whatever circumstances you
are in, and whoever you meet day by day, He is
pouring rivers of living water through you.

OSWALD CHAMBERS

June 13

May the road rise to meet you, may the wind always be at your back, the sun shine warm upon your face. . .and until we meet again, may God hold you in the palm of His hand.

IRISH BLESSING

Never put off until tomorrow
what you can avoid altogether.

If we weren't meant to keep starting over. . .
God wouldn't have granted us Monday.

July 21

I've gone to look for myself. If I should return before I get back, keep me here!

✻

The LORD will watch over your coming and going both now and forevermore.

PSALM 121:8 NIV

June 15

Stand outside this evening. Look at the stars.
Know that you are special and loved
by the One who created them.

July 20

For flowers that bloom about our feet,
Father, we thank You. For tender grass so fresh,
so sweet, Father, we thank You.

RALPH WALDO EMERSON

When things go wrong, as they sometimes will,
When the road you're trudging seems all uphill,
When the funds are low and the debts are high,
And you want to smile, but you have to sigh,
When care is pressing you down a bit,
Rest, if you must—but don't you quit!

July 19

What we see depends on what we are looking for.
Expect the best!

June 17

There is beauty in the forest
When the trees are green and fair,
There is beauty in the meadow
When the wildflowers scent the air.
There is beauty in the sunlight
and the soft blue beams above.
Oh, the world is full of beauty
when the heart is full of love.

July 18

"And why are you worried about clothing?
Observe how the lilies of the field grow;
they do not toil nor do they spin, yet I say
to you that not even Solomon in all his
glory clothed himself like one of these."

Matthew 6:28–29 NASB

June 18

If you treat others as if they were what they ought to be and could be, they will become what they ought to be and could be.

July 17

If a care is too small to be turned into a prayer,
it is too small to be made into a burden.

June 19

Enjoy today. . . . God loves
to hear your laughter.

July 16

A smile is contagious. Start an epidemic!

The human body was wisely designed—
we can neither pat our own backs
nor kick ourselves too easily.

July 15

What you are becoming is more important
than what you are accomplishing.

June 21

Lord, when I am wrong, help me to
be willing to change. And when I
am right. . .help me to be easy to live with.

Love is the reason
behind everything God does.

Happiness is found along the way,
not at the end of the road.

July 13

The sun. . .in its full glory, either at
rising or setting—this, and many
other like blessings we enjoy daily. . .
because they are so common, most men
forget to pay their praises. But let not us.

IZAAK WALTON

June 23

Do not just believe in
miracles—rely on them.

July 12

The greatest sweetener of
human life is friendship.

JOSEPH ADDISON

June 24

Even though on the outside it often looks like things are falling apart on us, on the inside, where God is making new life, not a day goes by without his unfolding grace.

2 CORINTHIANS 4:16 MSG

July 11

We always have the option to choose joy!

Yet I will rejoice in the Lord,
I will be joyful in God my Savior.

Habakkuk 3:18 niv

June 25

This is and has been the Father's work from the beginning—to bring us into the home of His heart.

GEORGE MACDONALD

The reason for loving God is God Himself,
and the measure in which we should love
Him is to love Him without measure.

BERNARD OF CLAIRVAUX

God created the world out of nothing,
and so long as we are nothing,
He can make something out of us.

MARTIN LUTHER

July 9

If you have a one-track mind. . .
make sure it's fixed on God.

June 27

Delight yourself in the surprises of today!

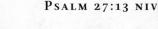

I am still confident of this: I will see the
goodness of the LORD in the land of the living.

PSALM 27:13 NIV

July 8

When we are kind to ourselves, we make ourselves a gift to those around us.

Count your age by friends, not years.
Count your life by smiles, not tears.

July 7

There will never be anyone like you.
Allowing God to fulfill His purpose in you
is the miracle for which you were created.

June 29

The happiest heart that ever beat
Was in some quiet breast
That found the common daylight sweet
And left to heaven the rest.

JOHN V. CHENEY

July 6

The world is a better place because
Noah didn't say, "I don't do arks."

By faith, Noah built a ship in the middle of
dry land. He was warned about something he
couldn't see, and acted on what he was told.

HEBREWS 11:7 MSG

❖❖❖❖❖❖❖❖❖❖❖❖❖❖❖❖❖❖❖❖❖❖❖❖❖❖❖❖❖

Worry less and work more. Ride less
and walk more. Frown less and laugh more.
Preach less and practice more.

July 5

Open the windows of our spirits and fill us full of light; open wide the door of our hearts that we may receive and entertain Thee with all the powers of our adoration.

CHRISTINA ROSSETTI

July 1

True greatness consists of
being great in little things.

"You have been faithful with a few things;
I will put you in charge of many things."

Matthew 25:21 niv

I adore simple pleasures. They
are the last refuge of the complex.

Oscar Wilde

July 2

The sunrise is God's greeting—the sunset, His signature.

July 3

Long may our land be
bright with freedom's holy light;
protect us by Thy might, Great God, our King!

FRANCIS SMITH